AFTER DARK

POEMS ABOUT NOCTURNAL ANIMALS

DAVID L. HARRISON

Illustrations by
STEPHANIE LABERIS

WORDSONG

AN IMPRINT OF BOYDS MILLS & KANE

New York

CONTENTS

THE REHEARSAL
(GRAY WOLF)

You wild thing.
You bouncy pup,
roughhousing
with your siblings.

Let the grown-ups
howl in the night,
keep your belly full,
hide you from eagles.

Play rambunctious games—
growly, pouncy, bitey games.
Time will come soon enough
to grow up, fight for life.

Time will come
when you and your mate
run the pack,
decide where to hunt,
hide your pups from eagles.

For now,
play tag,
pretend *grrr*,
pounce ferociously
on your siblings.

POSTED PROPERTY
(COUGAR)

Buries remains
of the deer
for later.

Pads on soft,
silent feet.

Leaves few clues
to where he's been.

6

Pauses,
scrapes pine needles
into a mound.
Sprays urine—
a signpost, a warning—
reminding others
where they should not be.

Belly full,
night's work done,
he rests.

MOUTH OF DOOM
(FLATHEAD CATFISH)

Defender of his nest,
protector of his eggs,
he holes up by day in sunken lair.

By night—
silent submarine,
solitary stalker,
his small eyes probe dark water.

Beware fish—
careless frog by river's edge—
slender snake
curving in moonlight—
his grim mouth opens wide
to swallow you down
his cavernous maw.

THE HUNT IS ON

(COYOTES)

Shhh, listen . . .
Hear that howling?
Out there in the dark?
Dogs don't howl,
not like that.

They're on the hunt.
Better take warning—
Be you mouse or deer, be watchful.
Coyotes are near.

9

DON'T LET HIM NEEDLE YOU
(PORCUPINE)

Eats shoots and leaves—
even bark.
If you hear him coming,
better hark.
You wouldn't want to bump him
in the dark.

He's a mind-his-own-business
kind of guy.
Would rather climb than walk,
rather shy,
but thirty thousand needles
testify
to thirty thousand reasons
to pass him by.

With tooth and needle fury—
a shocking sight—
he'll battle any rival
to gain the right
to approach a waiting female
in hopes she might
accept him as her mate
tonight.

NIGHT CLASS
(SKUNK)

Mama skunk
knows the story.
Never play
in an empty street.

Danger lurks
beyond the light,
in dark doorways,
behind trash cans,
around the corner.

Mama skunk
knows the story.
Never play
in an empty street.
The street is
never empty.

ARMORED NIGHT KNIGHT
(NINE-BANDED ARMADILLO)

At twilight ambles from his den,
armored as some ancient knight
with dagger claws, sets to work
gouging up the sod for worms,
maggots, grubs, scorpions, bugs.
Leaves a trail of pocked lawns
for angry owners come dawn.

12

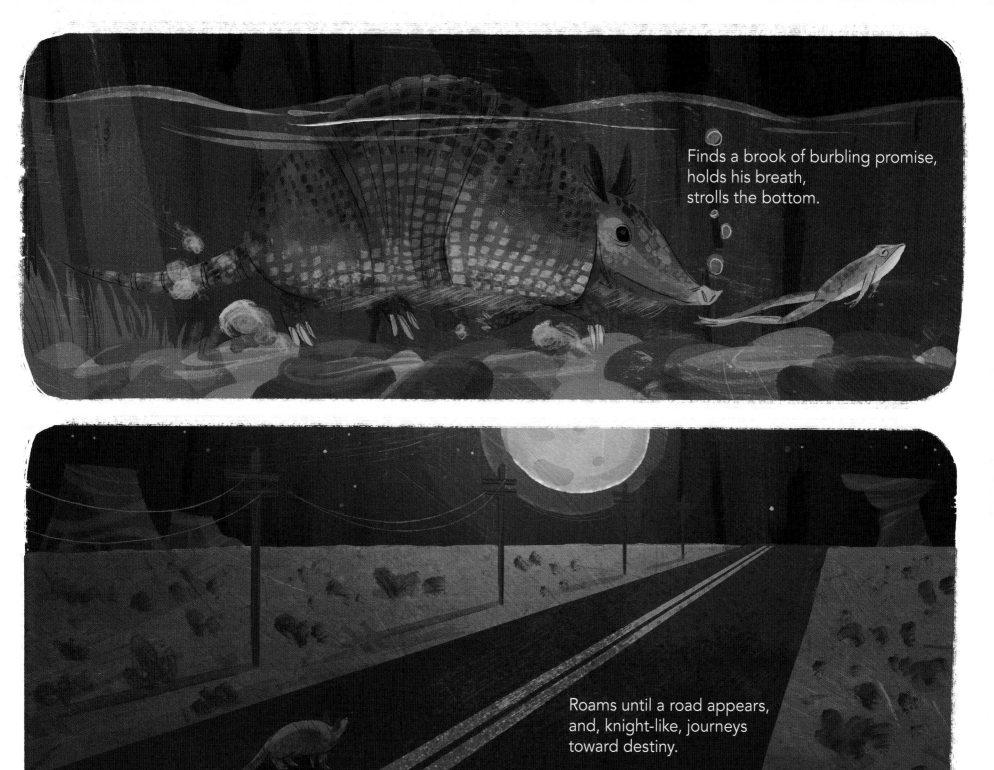

Finds a brook of burbling promise,
holds his breath,
strolls the bottom.

Roams until a road appears,
and, knight-like, journeys
toward destiny.

TOOTHY GRIN
(KIT FOX)

If you are mouse,
bird, rabbit . . .
If you are squirrel,
grasshopper, rat . . .

Beware when fox
emerges from the dark.
First you'll see the blackberry nose,
then the grin
that hides stiletto teeth.

Above the teeth,
luminous eyes,
ears like antennae tuned to you.
Behind the teeth,
luxurious coat,
glorious, bushy tail.

But all you'll see
of fox in the dark
are teeth,
teeth,
teeth.

OWL RULES
(SCREECH OWL)

Never work for food

Sit on your perch
with sleepy eye
till something creeps
or flutters by.

Eat whatever

Mice are nice, but so are bats,
worms, squirrels, tadpoles,
jays, doves, frogs, rats,
lizards, rabbits, moles . . .

16

Who needs a nest?

Don't waste effort
with twigs and thatch.
They're only eggs.
They're going to hatch.

Tease campers

If you time
your whistles right,
you'll keep them sleepless
half the night.

BUG PATROL

(MEXICAN FREE-TAILED BAT)

Bat awakes, knows
it's time to hunt, goes
in zigzag flight,
deserts cave
for dark night, swirls

into the sky, unfurls
like smoke,
a black cloak
on the air.

Bugs
beware.
Bat is there.

THE QUEEN
(LUNA MOTH)

Like regal monarch of the night
or fairy in the airy light,
richly robed in ermine white,
winged in velvet royal green.

Suitors you have never seen
find you here in woods serene.
You've much to do before the dawn
so when your fleeting life is gone,
future queens can carry on.

A NIGHT'S WORK
(DEER MOUSE)

Mouse creeps
without sound—
stops,
listens.

Sniffs dirt
between corn rows,
finds a kernel,
snatches it—
stops,
listens.

Owl's about,
stares for mouse—
Fox is out,
sniffs for mouse—
stop,
listen.

20

Cheeks bulging,
mouse races.
Owl plummets.
Fox strikes.

Talons rip.
Teeth snap
empty air.

Heart pounding,
mouse bounces
down his hole,
for now,
corn forgotten
in his cheeks.

THE KING
(MEXICAN RED-KNEE TARANTULA)

Leg
  by leg
    by leg
      by leg
        by leg
          by leg
            by leg
              by leg

you emerge from dark lair,
subterranean monster,
King Kong of spiders,
flexing fangs
like spears in the night,
moving off like black ink
oozing across the land,
ravenous for insect, frog,
unlucky toad to embrace.
Tonight almost anything will do.

IN A MOOD
(ARIZONA HAIRY SCORPION)

Holed up
in a burrow all day,
you prowl—
hungry.

Maybe a bug
won't be enough.
Might take a lizard.
Even your young
clinging to your back
aren't safe
when mama's hungry.

Stinger raised,
pinchers ready,
you enter the night.
Maybe a lizard
won't be enough.
Might take a mouse
when a scorpion prowls—
hungry.

BY LAND AND BY SEA
(LAND HERMIT CRAB)

Air-breather,
prisoner of land,
you cast your eggs
upon the sea.

Your young will hatch—
water creatures,
aliens to your world.

Duty done,
retreat to the woods,
try on vacant shells
for a better fit.

One day your young
will leave the sea,
breathe air like you,
live on land.
Not your concern.

SURVIVOR
(COCKROACH)

I ply my trade by shade of night,
creeping into holes and cracks,
prying after tasty snacks,
cautious, staying out of sight.
By day I find a place to rest,
a hidden nook, a safe retreat
away from claws and trampling feet
till darkness calls me from my nest.

I've much to do before the dawn.
Whatever you leave out is fair.
I'll find your food and have my share,
but when the light comes on, I'm gone.

HEAR THIS! HEAR THIS!
(SPRING PEEPERS)

The peepers are back!
The peepers are back!

    It's spring!

Soloists the size
of small leaves
clamor for mates
like miniature bells.

    It's spring!
    It's spring!

Jangling the night,
trilling romance.
There are bugs to eat.
There are eggs to lay.

    It's spring!
    It's spring!
    Time for love!

The night vibrates
with peep-peeping welcome:

    It's spring!
    It's spring!
    Time for love!

SLIMY CHARACTER
(LEOPARD SLUG)

Along a path of slime
you softly flow,
scraping holes in petals
as you go,
spoiling daffodil
and hollyhock.
Leaving a sticky line
across the walk,
glistening as mucus will
in morning light,
proof that you were here
by dark of night.

IN A HURRY!
(CRICKET)

The cricket has found
that he merrily sings—
when he rubs his wings—
a chirping sound.

His life isn't long,
so before it's too late,
he calls for a mate
with his crickety song.

INSECT TEXTING
(COMMON EASTERN FIREFLY)

Firefly flashes
polka dot the lawn.
Blinker off . . .
Blinker on.
Looking for a mate
before they're all gone.
Blinker off . . .
Blinker on.

Firefly females
watch from the grass,
checking each flash
as suitors pass.

Checking how bright,
how long it lasts,
firefly females
watch from the grass.

Firefly flashes
polka dot the lawn,
might find a mate
before they're all gone.
Blinker off . . .
Blinker on.

GRAY WOLF

- Hunts deer, elk, and moose, but will also hunt beavers, rabbits, and even eat carrion.
- As many as 17,000 dwell in Alaska and other northern parts of the United States.
- The whole pack pitches in to help look after the pups.
- Pups are born blind and deaf but are able to see and hear after about two weeks.

COUGAR

- Preys on deer, mountain goats, sheep, elk, and even moose.
- Is exceptionally strong and can leap thirty feet.
- Makes a range of sounds, from moans and wails to growls, chirps, and hisses.
- After mating, males go their own way. Kittens stay with their mother for a year or two.

FLATHEAD CATFISH

- Gulps down fish, small snakes, frogs, and anything else that fits into its huge mouth.
- Enormous males are three times heavier than a coyote.
- Females can lay up to 100,000 eggs at one time.
- Hatchlings, called fry, are common prey for fish and birds.

COYOTE

- Eats mice, rabbits, insects, birds, reptiles, frogs, fish, and fruit.
- Most adult pairs mate for life and raise their cubs together in dens dug in the ground or hollow trees.
- Individuals may hunt alone, but a family may sometimes band together to take down larger prey.
- Cubs are born blind; their eyes open after ten days. They reach adult size by nine months.

PORCUPINE

- Eats roots, bark, leaves, grass, nuts, and fruit.
- Quills are modified hairs with foam-filled shafts and barbed tips.
- During mating season, males battle over females, sometimes to the death. If a female flattens her quills, she has accepted a male's advances.
- Baby porcupines (porcupettes) are born with teeth and can walk.

SKUNK

- Digs for insects and small rodents, but will eat anything from fish to grass to carrion.
- When threatened, may hiss, grunt, click its teeth, and stamp its feet, but it is best known for the vile odor of its spray.
- Males have been known to eat their young.
- Babies (kits) are born blind and deaf, and are raised by their mothers.

NINE-BANDED ARMADILLO

- With sharp claws, digs for insects such as beetles, ants, and larvae to capture with its long, sticky tongue.
- Can carry bacteria that causes Hansen's disease (also called leprosy).
- Closest relatives are anteaters and sloths.
- After fertilization, the egg divides into four, so females always have identical quadruplets.

KIT FOX

- Prefers hunting for rodents and rabbits, but also likes insects, reptiles, and birds.
- Uses its famous bushy tail for balance and as a good nose-warmer on chilly nights.
- A lone hunter, stalks its prey and pounces like a cat.
- Pups remain in the den for the first month of their lives.

SCREECH OWL

- Eats mice, voles, insects, frogs, small snakes, and other birds.
- Instead of making nests, occupies whatever's handy — tree holes, wood piles, even mailboxes.
- Litters the ground with the pellets they throw up, containing bones, fur, and feathers from recent meals.
- Females usually lay three to five eggs in early spring. Young are ready to fly in four weeks.

MEXICAN FREE-TAILED BAT

- Eats moths and other insects — sometimes devouring as much as two-thirds its weight in prey.
- Sends out rapid high-pitched sounds that bounce back and tell it what and where the object is (echolocation).
- Bat droppings (guano) make good fertilizer and were once used in making gunpowder.
- Females give birth to one pup a year and nurse it for several weeks until it can fly and hunt.

LUNA MOTH

- Luna moths live for about a week and don't eat.
- In that time, a female must attract a male, mate, and lay eggs.
- Females release odors called pheromones that males can detect from miles away.
- Caterpillars hatch hungry. For a month they chew on leaves of walnut, hickory, sweet gum, and paper birch trees, then spin a cocoon. Three weeks later they emerge as adult moths.

R MOUSE

- Eats plants and animals, including insects, seeds, fruits, flowers, and nuts.
- On the menus of cats, foxes, coyotes, owls, hawks, eagles, crows, blue jays, herons, snakes, and many others.
- In twelve months, one mated pair and their offspring could make 8,000 mice!
- Young are born hairless, with wrinkled, pink skin, closed eyes, and folded-over ears. Thirty-five days later, the females can start having babies.

XICAN RED-KNEE TARANTULA

- Feeds on insects, millipedes, small toads, frogs, mice, and lizards.
- Venom liquefies prey so it can suck the juices through its tube-like mouth.
- The tarantula hawk wasp stings a tarantula to paralyze it, then buries it with an egg to feed the larva when it hatches.
- Female's egg sac may contain more than 200 spiderlings that hatch together.

ZONA HAIRY SCORPION

- Diet includes insects, spiders, lizards, other scorpions, including its own young.
- Related to ticks, mites, and spiders, and have been around for millions of years.
- Largest scorpion in North America.
- Females give live birth; babies ride on mama's back until they are ready to survive on their own.

ND HERMIT CRAB

- Feeds on algae, dead animals, and other crabs.
- Adults have gills and must remain close to water to keep them moist, yet would drown if submerged.
- Wears deserted snail shells to protect its soft undersides.
- Baby crabs hatch from eggs the female places in the sea.

ERICAN COCKROACH

- Eats almost anything—pastries, book bindings, hair, leather, beer, fermenting foods.
- Spreads at least twenty-seven kinds of human diseases and parasites.
- One of the fastest running insects on earth; has been timed at 3.4 miles per hour.
- Young, called nymphs, hatch from eggs and grow by shedding their skins. They reach adulthood in a few weeks.

SPRING PEEPERS

- Prefer dining on spiders, ants, flies, and beetles.
- A chorus of mating calls can be heard more than two miles away.
- Good at hiding behind loose bark, in leaves, or on rocks beside water.
- Females deposit around 1,000 eggs in water. When tadpoles hatch, they're on their own.

LEOPARD SLUG

- Feeds on dead plants, fungus, feces, carrion, and other slugs.
- To keep from drying out, travels by night and prefers tunnels and cool, damp places.
- In spite of its slimy body, it is eaten by turtles, toads, birds, and beetles.
- Can lay up to 200 eggs. Young reach maturity in two years.

CRICKET

- Eats anything from fruits and seeds to ants and aphids to dead insects, including crickets.
- Males chirp by rubbing their outer wings together.
- Females hear them through special eardrums located in their front legs.
- Babies hatch in about two weeks and become adults in about a month, shedding and eating their skins until they develop wings.

COMMON EASTERN FIREFLY

- Eats snails, worms, and insects—including other fireflies.
- It's not a fly, it's a beetle.
- To most animals, fireflies taste terrible so predators learn to leave them alone.
- When the young larva hatches, it usually lives in the ground and eats slugs, snails, and worms.

RACCOON

- Likes fruits, nuts, corn, insects, rodents, frogs, eggs, and crayfish, but will also eat easy meals from picnic scraps, dog food bowls, and trash cans.
- Usually den in trees or abandoned burrows, but a cozy attic will do fine.
- Can run fifteen miles an hour and shimmy up or down a tree headfirst or tailfirst.
- Females raise the young, called kits.

To Sneed and Maridel Niederriter, with love and good memories
   —DLH

To the hardworking staff and volunteers at the Lindsay Wildlife
Rehabilitation Hospital for helping all creatures of the night who
are in need —SL

ACKNOWLEDGMENTS

The author and illustrator thank Paul Beier, John Capinera, Marty Crump, Brian Cypher,
Pam Fuller, Stan Gehrt, Joseph Lapp, Buck Mangipane, Colleen McDonough, Timothy
Pearce, John Rappole, Robert Raven, Uldis Roze, Warren Savary, and Christopher Tudge
for their careful review of the text and illustrations.

WordSong
An Imprint of Boyds Mills & Kane
wordsongpoetry.com
Printed in China

ISBN: 978-1-62979-717-5
Library of Congress Control Number: 2019904392

First edition
10 9 8 7 6 5 4 3 2 1

The text is set in Avenir.
The titles are set in Nickname.
The illustrations are digital.